Lerner SPORTS

SPORTS ALL-STARS

LUKA DONCIC

Jon M. Fishman

Lerner Publications ◆ Minneapolis

Lerner Publications Company
An imprint of Lerner Publishing Group, Inc.
241 First Avenue North
Minneapolis, MN 55401 USA

For reading levels and more information, look up this title at www.lernerbooks.com.

Main body text set in Albany Std 22. Typeface provided by Agfa.

Editor: Shee Yang **Designer:** Susan Fienhage

Library of Congress Cataloging-in-Publication Data

Names: Fishman, Jon M., author.
Title: Luka Doncic / Jon M. Fishman.
Description: Minneapolis, MN : Lerner Publications, 2021 | Series: Sports all-stars (Lerner sports) | Includes bibliographical references and index. | Audience: Ages 7–11 | Audience: Grades 4–6 | Summary: "Could the Dallas Mavericks have another European wonder in Luka Doncic? The Slovenian basketball extraordinaire hit the professional court with a bang! Readers will keep turning pages to learn about this star in the making"— Provided by publisher.
Identifiers: LCCN 2019046365 (print) | LCCN 2019046366 (ebook) | ISBN 9781541597525 (library binding) | ISBN 9781728401010 (ebook)
Subjects: LCSH: Doncic, Luka—Juvenile literature. | Basketball players—Slovenia—Biography—Juvenile literature. | Dallas Mavericks (Basketball team)—History—Juvenile literature.
Classification: LCC GV884.D63 F57 2021 (print) | LCC GV884.D63 (ebook) | DDC 796.323092 [B]—dc23

LC record available at https://lccn.loc.gov/2019046365
LC ebook record available at https://lccn.loc.gov/2019046366

Manufactured in the United States of America
1-47856-48296-4/2/2020

CONTENTS

DONCIC'S TIME

Doncic and Dirk Nowitzki (*left*) greet each other on the court before a game on March 26, 2019.

Luka Doncic (LOO-kuh DON-chitch) was one of the hottest young players in the National Basketball Association (NBA). In 2018–2019, his **rookie** season, he averaged more than 21 points per game (PPG) for the Dallas Mavericks. But on April 9, 2019, fans were buzzing about Doncic's teammate, Dirk Nowitzki. The game against the Phoenix Suns was the final home game of Nowitzki's career. He planned to retire after the season.

- **Date of birth:** February 28, 1999
- **Position:** guard and forward
- **League:** National Basketball Association (NBA)
- **Professional highlights:** won the EuroLeague championship in 2018 with Real Madrid; chosen third overall in the 2018 NBA Draft; won the 2018–2019 NBA Rookie of the Year award
- **Personal highlights:** trained with NBA superstar Stephen Curry before Doncic's rookie season; is one of the league's most popular players with fans; was one of the subjects of the documentary *Something in the Water*, which follows his journey to the NBA

Nowitzki was beloved by Dallas fans. He played 21 seasons in the NBA, all of them with the Mavericks. When Dallas won the NBA Finals in 2011, Nowitzki won the Finals Most Valuable Player (MVP) Award. But with Nowitzki set to retire in 2019, Doncic naturally started to become the team's leader.

Doncic and the Mavericks rolled over the Suns in the first half. With less than two minutes left in the second quarter, Doncic launched a long **jump shot**. A Suns player committed a **foul** against Doncic, but the shot was good. Doncic made a **free throw** to give Dallas a huge 68–36 lead.

Nowitzki playing his last home game before retirement in 2019

In the second half, the Suns came roaring back. They outscored the Mavericks by 11 points in the third quarter. In the fourth quarter, Dallas held a four-point lead with about three and a half minutes left. That's when Dallas's rising new leader stepped up.

Doncic launched a long arcing shot from behind the three-point line. *Swish!* When Dallas got the ball again, Justin Jackson scored with an **assist** from Doncic. Then Doncic hit another long three-pointer to give the Mavericks a 13-point lead. He had helped his team score eight points in just over one minute. The Suns couldn't catch up, and Dallas won the game 120–109.

Doncic averaged more than 21 PPG during his rookie season.

Doncic scored 21 points in the game. He added 11 assists and 16 **rebounds** for his eighth **triple-double** of the season. With Nowitzki retiring, Doncic had big shoes to fill. But Mavericks coach Rick Carlisle thought Doncic was up to the task. "[Doncic is] the best rookie I've seen since LeBron James, Larry Bird, Magic Johnson, and Michael Jordan," he said.

FATHER'S FOOTSTEPS

Sasa Doncic (*right*) plays Polish team Trefl Sopot in Game 7 of the EuroLeague Basketball Finals on December 6, 2007.

Luka Doncic first picked up a basketball when he was seven months old. The sport was the family business, and Luka loved it. His father, Sasa (Sa-sha), played pro basketball in Slovenia. In 2008, Sasa's team, Union Olimpija, won the Slovenian League championship.

Slovenia

As a young boy, Luka attended almost all of his father's games. He sat behind one of the baskets. At halftime, he took to the floor to shoot jump shots.

Goran Dragic was Sasa's teammate in Slovenia and played in the NBA. Dragic remembers watching Luka shoot baskets during halftime. "Even at that age you could see he had a great feeling for the ball like his dad," Dragic said. Luka's dad was a smart, skillful player. He had a flashy style, and his teammates were drawn to him as a leader. Sasa passed on what he could to Luka, but it would be Luka's own drive and love for the game that would bring him to the NBA.

According to his family, by the time Luka was one, he was making shots in the miniature hoop his parents put in his room.

At the age of seven, Luka began playing for his school's basketball team in Ljubljana. The next year, his father joined Union Olimpija. The team ran a basketball school, and they asked Luka to practice with other players his age.

About 15 minutes into his first practice with Olimpija, coaches pulled Luka aside. They told him he was too good to practice with players his own age. The coaches moved Luka to a group of older kids. For the next few years, Luka practiced and played against kids three or four years older than he was.

At the age of 13, Luka moved to Spain to join Real Madrid's training program. The best players move up and eventually join Real Madrid's pro team. Just as he had done in Ljubljana, Luka competed against older players.

In 2014, Luka played his first pro game with Real Madrid. Just past his 16th birthday, Luka was the youngest person to ever play for the team. His teammates were amazed by the skill he had at such a young age.

Luka kept improving. In 2017–2018, he led Real Madrid to the EuroLeague championship. He won the league's MVP and Final Four MVP awards. The NBA took notice, and they were ready for him.

Doncic celebrates winning the EuroLeague on May 20, 2018.

PLAYING WEIGHT

Doncic with NBA commissioner Adam Silver after being drafted in 2018

Doncic is officially listed by the NBA at 6 feet 7 inches (2 m) tall and 218 pounds (99 kg). But when the 2018–2019 season began, he looked heavier than usual. That's the way the Mavericks wanted it.

At 6 feet 7 inches (2 m), Doncic is about 3 inches (7.6 cm) taller than the league's average shooting guard.

When Doncic arrived in the United States in the summer of 2018, he had just finished playing a year of basketball with Real Madrid. In preparation for the NBA, his new Dallas coaches wanted him to rest. So Doncic took it easy for a month and gained some weight.

Doncic during a game against the New Orleans Pelicans on December 5, 2018

As the beginning of his first NBA season drew near, Doncic started to work out. In August, he met superstar Stephen Curry for a training session. Curry has won two NBA MVP awards and three NBA championships with the Golden State Warriors. Doncic and Curry did **drills** together for three hours. They dribbled, shot, moved quickly to new positions, and shot again. They ran down the court, each dribbling a ball in either hand. In one drill, Doncic and Curry each dribbled a basketball with one hand while bouncing a tennis ball off the wall with the other.

Doncic warming up before a game against the Brooklyn Nets on March 4, 2019

Doncic guards Curry in the first quarter of a game in Oakland, California, on December 22, 2018.

Dribbling drills help players control the ball in tricky situations. Doncic learned how much work it takes to be a superstar like Curry. Becoming an NBA MVP takes talent, practice, and a lot of time in the gym.

After his rookie season, Doncic set out to lose weight. He posted photos of himself on social media doing exercises such as the **trap bar** carry. He lifted a heavy trap bar and held it at his sides. Then he carried it to the

Working out off the court helps Doncic avoid feeling tired during games.

Doncic makes sure he has stretched before playing to prevent injuries.

end of a course and back. The move built muscle all over Doncic's body.

By the start of the 2019–2020 season, Doncic had lost about 20 pounds (9 kg). He said the weight loss made him faster on the court. The rest of the NBA would have to try to keep up.

"LUKAMANIA"

Doncic greets fans after a game in Houston, Texas, on November 24, 2019.

When stars arrive at airports, they're often surrounded by fans. People want selfies, autographs, and hugs. Fans usually don't swarm rookies before they've even been drafted. But they did swarm Doncic when he arrived in New York City for the NBA Draft on June 20, 2018.

US basketball fans knew all about Doncic from his success in Europe. Rumors swirled around which team would take him in the draft. The Sacramento Kings, Memphis Grizzlies, and other teams were all said to be interested in him. On draft day, the Atlanta Hawks chose Doncic with the third overall pick. That same day, Atlanta traded him to Dallas.

Doncic poses with EuroLeague fans before a game against the New Orleans Pelicans on December 5, 2018.

Doncic congratulates Nowitzki after Nowitzki completes a basket to become the sixth all-time leading scorer in the NBA.

Doncic was thrilled to join the Mavericks. He was especially excited to play with Nowitzki. "He's a great leader and I'm just happy to be part of his career and want to learn as much as I can," Doncic said. "I am excited to be part of the Dallas family."

Two-Sport Star

In September 2019, Doncic showed off his court skills—on a tennis court. Each year the Chris Evert Pro-Celebrity Tennis Classic raises money to help children around the world improve their health, education, and more. Before the event, Doncic said that he wasn't a good tennis player. But he wanted to help.

Doncic proved to be a better player than he had admitted. He put on a show for fans and spent time signing autographs. He even posted photos and videos of himself playing tennis on social media.

Chris Evert was one of the world's top tennis players before she retired from the sport in 1989.

The film *Something in the Water* details Doncic's time playing in Europe.

Soon after the draft, NBA on TNT released a documentary about Doncic's life. *Something in the Water* follows Doncic and Dzanan Musa, an NBA player from Bosnia and Herzegovina. The film covers Doncic's journey from Slovenia to Spain to the United States. It also highlights the rapid growth of his basketball skills.

After seeing the movie, Mavericks fans were even more excited to see Doncic on the court. As the team traveled for games in 2018–2019, fans made their interest clear. They waited for Doncic outside arenas and buses, holding jerseys and posters for him to sign. Nowitzki had a special word for the fan excitement. "Lukamania is real," he said. "We're living it every day."

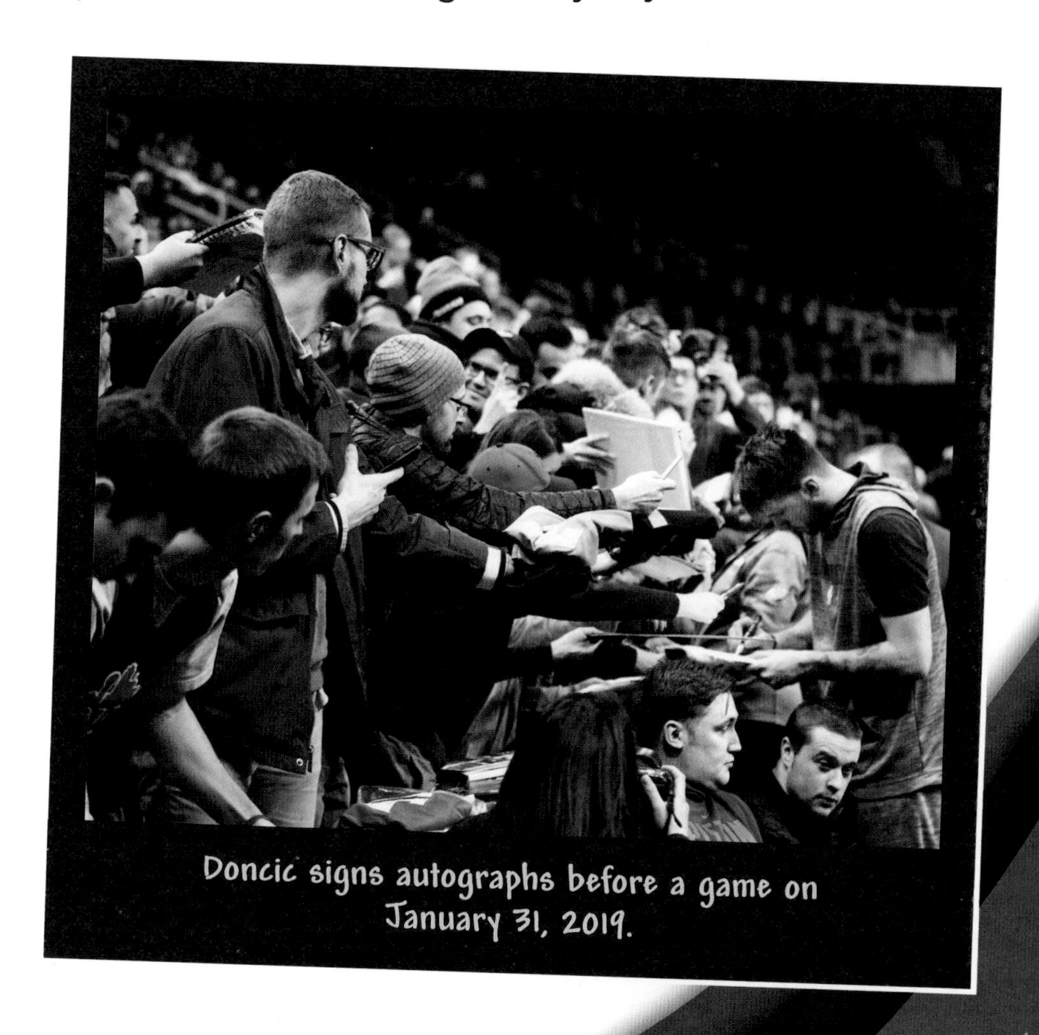

Doncic signs autographs before a game on January 31, 2019.

GOING HIGHER

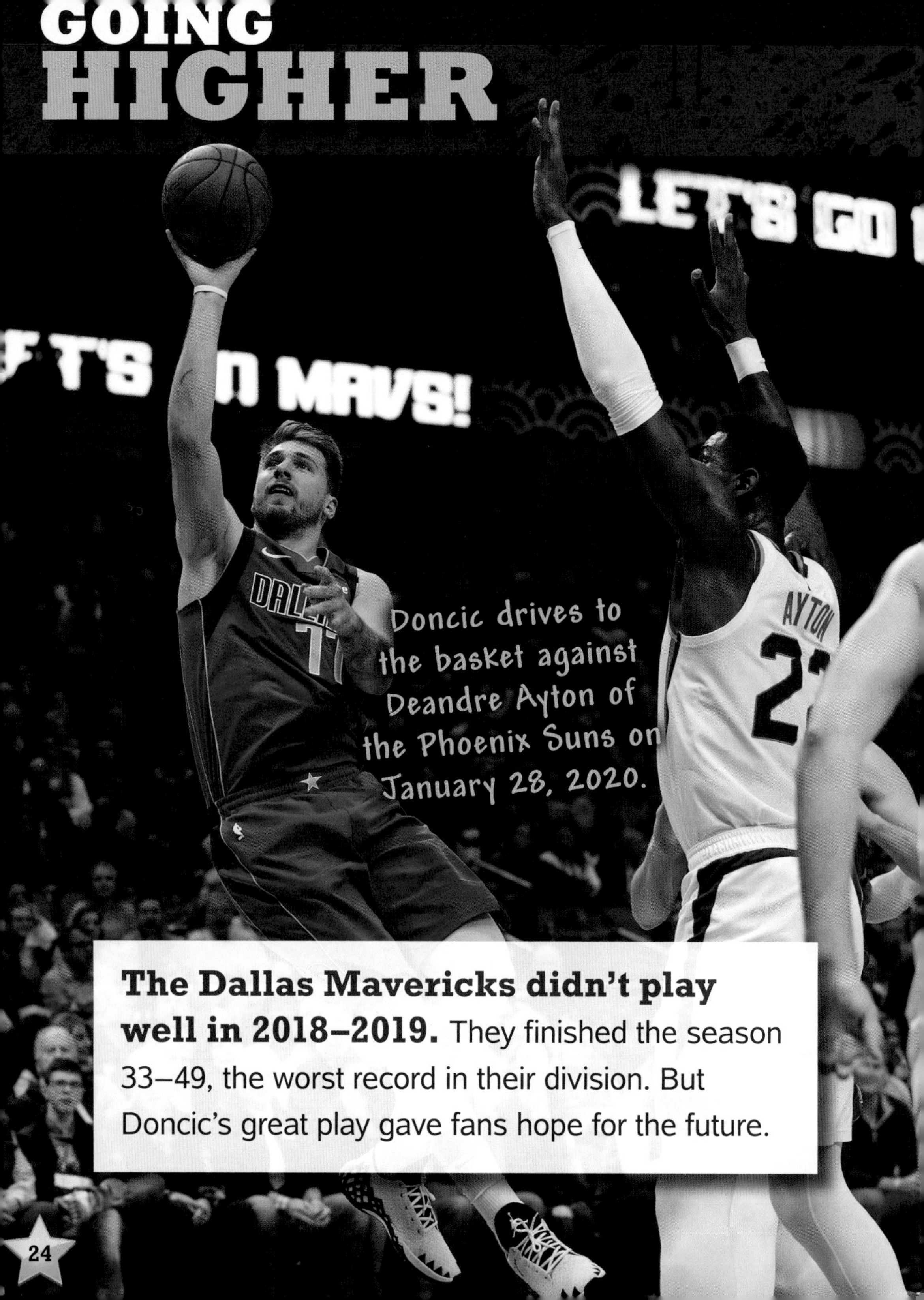

Doncic drives to the basket against Deandre Ayton of the Phoenix Suns on January 28, 2020.

The Dallas Mavericks didn't play well in 2018–2019. They finished the season 33–49, the worst record in their division. But Doncic's great play gave fans hope for the future.

Doncic receives the Western Conference Rookie of the Month award on December 12, 2018.

Doncic started out hot and never cooled off. He won the Rookie of the Month award every month of the season. That made him the obvious choice to win the Rookie of the Year award too.

Doncic received more than four million votes to play in the 2019 All-Star Game. Only superstars LeBron James and Giannis Antetokounmpo received more votes. Doncic's scoring, passing, and rebounding stats are amazing. They're some of the best ever for a player so young.

Giannis Antetokounmpo (left) challenges LeBron James at the 2019 NBA All-Star Game on February 17.

Doncic attempts a jump shot during a game on February 2, 2019, in Cleveland, Ohio.

Doncic had an incredible rookie season. But he wants to win the NBA championship. To reach his goal, he knows he must raise his stats even higher. “Everything must go higher,” Doncic said. “That’s what I’m looking for.”

All-Star Stats

Some players are great scorers, while others excel at rebounding or passing. The game's biggest stars can do it all. Take a look at where Doncic ranked in triple-doubles for his NBA rookie season.

Most Triple-Doubles in the NBA, 2018–2019

Player	Triple-Doubles
Russell Westbrook	34
Nikola Jokic	12
Ben Simmons	10
LeBron James	8
Luka Doncic	8
James Harden	7
Elfrid Payton	6
Giannis Antetokounmpo	5
Delon Wright	3

Source Notes

7 Brad Townsend, "Life after Dirk . . ." *Dallas Morning News*, April 11, 2019, https://www.dallasnews.com/sports/mavericks/2019/04/12/life-after-dirk-how-mavericks-luka-doncic-plan-to-fill-leadership-void-left-by-nowitzki/.

9 Mike Schmitz, "There Has Never Been an NBA Draft Prospect like Slovenia's Luka Doncic," ESPN, October 4, 2017, https://www.espn.com/nba/story/_/id/20668236/there-never-nba-draft-prospect-slovenia-luka-doncic.

20 Eddie Sefko, "Inside How the Mavs Got Their Top Target in Luka Doncic and Where They Go from Here," *Dallas Morning News*, June 29, 2018, https://www.dallasnews.com/sports/mavericks/2018/06/30/inside-how-the-mavs-got-their-top-target-in-luka-doncic-and-where-they-go-from-here/.

23 Marc Stein, "Luka Doncic Is a Sore Loser. He Is Also a Sensation," *New York Times*, February 27, 2019, https://www.nytimes.com/2019/02/27/sports/luka-doncic-dallas-mavericks.html.

27 Eddie Sefko, "Luka's Encore Will Be Tantalizing . . . ," NBA, Dallas Mavericks, September 30, 2019, https://www.mavs.com/lukas-encore-will-be-tantalizing-so-how-long-before-the-rising-star-becomes-full-blown-superstar/.

Glossary

assist: a pass that leads to a score

drills: exercises to improve skills

foul: breaking the rules of basketball

free throw: an unchallenged shot from behind the free throw line that is sometimes awarded when the other team commits a foul

jump shot: jumping into the air and releasing the ball with one or both hands at the peak of the jump

rebounds: recovering the ball after a missed shot

rookie: a first-year player

trap bar: a weight-training tool that uses multiple bars joined together to lift weights. It is also called a hex bar.

triple-double: when a player reaches 10 or more in three stats categories in one game

Further Information

Dallas Mavericks
https://www.mavs.com/

Jr. NBA
https://jr.nba.com/

Levit, Joe. *Basketball's G.O.A.T.: Michael Jordan, LeBron James, and More*. Minneapolis: Lerner Publications, 2020.

Luka Doncic
https://www.nba.com/players/luka/doncic/1629029

Monnig, Alex. *Luka Doncic: Basketball Star*. Lake Elmo, MN: Focus Readers, 2020.

Savage, Jeff. *Basketball Super Stats*. Minneapolis: Lerner Publications, 2018.

Index

Photo Acknowledgments

Image credits: Tom Pennington/Getty Images, pp. 4, 5, 20, 24; Omar Vega/Getty Images, p. 6; Christian Petersen/Getty Images, p. 7; Ales Fevzer/Getty Images, p. 8; Lukas Kurka/Shutterstock.com, p. 9; ANDREJ ISAKOVIC/AFP/Getty Images, p. 11; Mike Stobe/Getty Images, p. 12; Sean Gardner/Getty Images, p. 13; Matteo Marchi/Getty Images, p. 14; Jane Tyska/Digital First Media/The Mercury News/ Getty Images, p. 15; Jonathan Daniel/Getty Images, p. 16; Emilio Cobos/Euroleague Basketball/Getty Images, p. 17; Tim Warner/Getty Images, p. 18; Sean Gardner/ Getty Images, p. 19; Jason Koerner/Getty Images, p. 21; COOLMedia/Peter Sabok/ NurPhoto/Getty Images, p. 22; Cassy Athena/Getty Images, p. 23; Ronald Martinez/ Getty Images, p. 25; David T. Foster III/Charlotte Observer/Tribune News Service/ Getty Images, p. 26; Jason Miller/Getty Images, p. 27.

Cover image: Jim McIsaac/Getty Images.